# A Spot In My Heart

### Loving a Special Needs Dog

## Kelly Artieri

All rights reserved. No part of this publication may be reproduced, stored in a retrieval system, or transmitted, in any form or by any means, electronic, mechanical, photocopying, recording, or otherwise, without the written prior permission of the author.

Copyright © 2016 by Kelly Artieri
All rights reserved.

A Spot in My Heart/Kelly Artieri
ISBN: 978-1-946446-04-6
Ebook: 978-1-946446-05-3

For My Beautiful Boys
*Spot & Vinnie*

# Contents

| | |
|---|---|
| Hello | 1 |
| Never Again | 3 |
| A Bit of History | 7 |
| Color Genetics | 11 |
| Vinnie Comes Home | 15 |
| Who Trained Whom? | 19 |
| Testing Boundaries | 25 |
| Bad Dogs | 31 |
| He Loves Me, He Loves Me Not | 35 |
| Obsessive Compulsive Disorder | 39 |
| Doggie Day Care | 43 |
| Oh My! | 49 |
| Pica—Huh? | 53 |
| Round Two | 55 |
| Complications | 57 |
| Nothing Smaller Than a Beach Towel | 63 |
| Normality? | 67 |
| The Terrible Twos | 71 |
| Favorite Spots | 75 |
| Stranger Danger | 77 |
| For the Love of Vinnie! | 81 |
| Returning the Favor | 89 |
| What Goes Up Must Come Down | 93 |
| Everything Happens for a Reason | 99 |

**American Kennel Club (AKC):** A registry of purebred dog pedigrees in the United States.

**Baer Hearing Test:** The hearing test known as the brainstem auditory evoked response detects electrical activity in the cochlea and auditory pathways in the brain.

**Bilateral Deafness:** Deafness in which both ears are affected.

**Merle Gene:** Creates mottled patches of color in a solid or piebald coat and can affect skin pigment as well. Health issues are more typical and more severe when two merles are bred together.

**Obsessive Compulsive Disorder (OCD):** The presenting of exaggerations of normal dog behaviors.

**Pica:** A medical issue referring to eating non-food items.

**Piebald:** An animal that has a pattern of pigmented spots on an unpigmented (white) background of hair.

## Hello

My name is Kelly. I own a Dalmatian named Vinnie. Vinnie is deaf. Vinnie has made a spot in my heart and changed my life forever.

This is not another book about a superhuman dog named after a Reggae singer or one of those gut-wrenching stories that will leave you in a sobbing heap at the end. It is also not a handbook or a how-to manual. It is the story of Vinnie and my family that will only touch a select few. It might not be bestseller material, but it will hopefully help some people who challenge themselves to be where I was, where I often found myself alone. Vinnie was born bilaterally deaf; he also developed Pica and OCD.

I am not a veterinarian, nor am I a dog trainer or any kind of animal professional. I am just a normal—using that term loosely—average Joe who loves dogs and welcomes them into my life. When faced with the decision to accept a special needs dog into my home, I made the statement, "How hard can it be if you love them lots?" I will be quoting that statement many times throughout my writing. How little I knew, at the time, how very ironic that statement would be.

I looked for manuals, documents, periodicals, people—anything or anyone who could give me information on where to start. There were a few books, a couple of blog sites, and some amazing people, but I found very little to prepare me and my family for the task we had just undertaken.

That is my goal here: to compile the notes and journals I kept about the path I chose to take. I am sure some professionals may disagree or find fault with some of the things I did or didn't do, but most of us are not professional dog people. We just love them lots. If my words help one family or one dog, then it was worth the time to write them down.

My story is about my special needs Dalmatian. Many of my statistics and storylines will be specific to him, but take my words and insert your dog, your family, or your situation, and you will find many similarities. The advice in these pages could help with some of the special needs and hurdles you may be facing.

If you are blessed with a healthy dog without any of these handicaps, please enjoy my stories and hug your dog a bit closer. I am hopeful that my stories will make you laugh, make you shake your head, and motivate you to try my suggestions. You might even get creative and expand upon my ideas to make your life easier. I made mistakes and could have done many things better; you will too. My family and I learned as we went and did the best we could. I firmly believe we did all right, and I am pretty sure Vinnie thought so, too.

The one thing to always remember is that there is no definitive right way. There is only the way that works for you and your dog; but most importantly, love them lots.

## Never Again

There are 332 different breeds of dogs recognized by the World Canine Organization. We all have our favorites, from small and fluffy to big and active. Dog people gravitate to that comfortable place that usually has a furry face. They become our best friends. We make them part of our families. We cry when they hurt, and we swear we will never do it again when we lose them. But after a bit of time, most of us need to fill that emptiness they leave, and we jump right back in.

Spot was my first Dalmatian. He was my best friend for fourteen years. I lost him to cancer and severe arthritis due to years of leaping small buildings at a hundred miles an hour. That is a fairly typical Dalmatian activity. I have had many dogs and pets throughout my life, but I have never grieved like I did when I lost Spot. Like so many other dog owners, I said I would "never again" get another pet because it hurt too much to lose them.

A year or so after Spot was gone, I was visiting my sister, who was the director of a prominent Pet Rescue organization in Chicago. While visiting her facility, I met a Dalmatian that had been there for quite a while but just never seemed to get adopted. Seymour had a history of getting so excited when families came to visit that he scared them away. I sat with him for a long time. We had a deep discussion on how to behave when visitors came and other top-secret Dal stuff—or at least that was the excuse I used to cover the fact that I so desperately missed those sloppy kisses and slimy dog nose attentions. I missed Spot. I had been kidding myself that I was fine with not having a dog.

I finally admitted that I was truly a dog person and needed a dog in my life. More than that, I was a Dalmatian person. I loved their quirky personalities and their high energy. That was that. I went gleefully into the rescue site the following day to adopt Seymour. To my disappointment and excitement, Seymour had been adopted earlier that day. My sister and I laughed, saying it was thanks to the conversation I'd had with Seymour the previous day, since I obviously spoke fluent Dalmatian.

I liked the idea of adopting, so I began looking at a couple of Dalmatian rescue sites in my area. I filled out the application forms and waited. I thought I was the perfect candidate.

Nothing . . . No response, no interview, no contact. I was disappointed, but I chalked it off to the fact that, unfortunately, some things are just not meant to be.

Time went on, and I happened upon an advertisement quite by accident. It was a rather generic ad about Dal puppies expected in a few months with a phone number to call. I called and spoke with an amazing breeder. After a few minutes, I felt like I had known her forever.

During the course of our initial interview conversation, we discovered that the sire of my beloved Spot was the great-great-grandfather of her Dal mother to be. This must have been meant to be. The decision was made right then. I was going to have the chance to continue to enjoy the bloodline of my best friend.

I met with her several times and met her dogs. After conferring with my family, I reserved a future male puppy from her litter. "Never again" became any day now!

The happy day came, and four puppies were born: three girls and a boy. It was fate. That boy would be mine in about eight weeks. The breeder provided weekly photos so we would not miss a moment of our new puppy's growth, and my family and I had the pleasure of meeting and holding him at intervals for the first eight weeks when puppies must stay with the litter. The breeder explained that the puppies would be BAER hearing tested between five and six weeks, a requirement for Dalmatian puppies, put into effect by the American Kennel Club (AKC). There was nothing to worry about. It was just a formality. Vinnie was an active, healthy guy.

The phone call came. The words were difficult to find, and the news was not good. Our Vinnie was bilaterally deaf.

The breeder tearfully apologized and promised to help us find a new litter with another breeder. After the initial shock wore off, I asked her what would happen to the puppy. She explained that it was the formal policy and recommendation of the AKC that the pup be destroyed. She, of course, would attempt to find it a home.

Destroyed? Wait one minute! That is just not a word that should be used in the same sentence with the word "puppy." This five-week-old puppy that my family and I had held, had researched names for as carefully as was done for my daughter over twenty years ago—this "I'm never doing it again" dog that was Spot's kin—was not going to be destroyed! He had been our dog since before he was born.

Then, I said it.

"I will take him," I told the breeder. "I will learn how to care for him. After all, how hard could it be? My family and I will love him lots!"

Vinnie was a purebred Dalmatian and fully pedigreed, but he now had a big, black mark on his paperwork that prohibited him from mating or participating in any reindeer games or competitions. In the dog world, it is perfectly fine to discriminate against handicapped dogs. I signed a waiver that I would neuter him as soon as possible, so the deaf traits could not be passed along. We were fine with the rules. We weren't looking for a perfect dog. We were looking for Vinnie.

I got my wish, too; I was able to rescue a Dalmatian. After all, how hard could it be to raise a deaf dog if you loved him lots?

Though deafness can touch any breed of dog, my adventures were actually shared in part with both of my Dalmatians. Spot became almost deaf close to the end of his life, as many older dogs do. Now that you know how I got where I am, I will further explain how the planets aligned.

## A Bit of History

Of course, when you first think of a Dalmatian, you think of the standard Walt Disney version of *101 Dalmatians*. The original animated feature film debuted in movie theaters in 1961. It was a box office hit. The screen was adorned with adorable, black-and-white spotted puppies in cartoon animation. The movie was released to theaters again and again at strategic intervals throughout the years to keep children and families in love with the pups. Few kids did not recognize those silly, spotted faces.

In 1996, a live-action remake of *101 Dalmatians* was released featuring real actors and real dogs. Needless to say, the movie's popularity steamrolled and the love for the spotted hounds snowballed into pandemonium. Children everywhere wanted a "Pongo" or a "Perdita!" Breeders went wild with supply and demand for Dalmatians.

Unfortunately, thanks to demand, many problems arose due to overbreeding, inappropriate breeding, and the basic lack of owner understanding for this extremely high-maintenance breed and its nature. Many Dals were left homeless and in shelters when families could not handle their exuberant personalities or the health problems resulting from negligence during the breeding processes. No one blames Walt Disney or the conscientious breeder; those to blame are the ones who benefitted financially at the cost of the breed and the individual dogs. In fact, that is the very reason the AKC and many breeders took such a firm stand on improving the health and temperament of Dalmatians, damaged by the overpopulation problem. The gene pool needed to be cleaned up.

This very scenario can be found in many breeds of the new "designer" dogs. Every dog show features beautiful, well-behaved breeds from all over the world. If that breed or size of dog is not carefully researched and discussed with families prior to making the commitment, many of the same issues can arise. Not every dog is the right fit for all of us.

You would think that this concept would be common sense, but you would be surprised how many people react out of spontaneity—thus putting the dog at risk. Those dogs often find themselves relinquished to rescue sites or wandering the streets. Puppy mills and amateur breeders complicate the lives of many families and dogs. For some reason, they seem to think the rules just don't apply to them. It is all about the money.

Unfortunately, overly zealous breeding adds to that problem and also exaggerates any flaws that exist in bloodlines. This is true for all breeds. I can talk in detail about the Dalmatian breed, since it is the one I know best. A closer look will help to define their nature and the flaws that come along with the variances that make a Dalmatian a Dalmatian.

The Dalmatian breed is known as "coach dogs" or "fire dogs" because they ran beside the horses of fire carriages to keep the horses calm and to protect their legs from injury by predators. They love to run long and fast. Their sleek physique and beautiful markings have always been admired, and many a head has turned when one of these majestic dogs goes by. Of course, the AKC has a breed standard for Dals, but the abridged version—since this is not meant to be a technical manual about Dalmatians—is that Dalmatians come in a couple of different flavors. The Dal coat is either black and white or brown (liver) and white-spotted. Their eyes can be brown, blue, or a combination of both. They are medium-sized dogs that range between forty-five and sixty-five pounds and live between twelve and fourteen years.

## Color Genetics

I know that statistics are not the most exciting reading, and they are often difficult to understand. Trust me; I am not giving a very deep scientific theory, just a basic encyclopedia-type overview. I am no expert. Remember, I am just a dog parent like you, but as a dog owner, this is part of the research you should do just to understand and appreciate who your dog is and why he could have special needs.

An article written by Dr. George M. Strain from Louisiana State University Comparative Biomedical Sciences School of Veterinary Medicine reads, "Congenital deafness has been reported for approximately eighty-five breeds. It can potentially appear in any breed but especially those with white pigmentation. Two pigmentation genes in particular are often associated with deafness in dogs: the merle gene (seen in the Collie, Shetland Sheepdog, Dappled Dachshund, Harlequin Great Dane, American Foxhound, Old English Sheepdog, and Norwegian Dunker Hound among others) and the piebald gene (Bull Terrier, Samoyed, Greyhound, Great Pyrenees, Sealyham Terrier, Beagle, Bulldog, Dalmatian, and English Setter). The deafness, which usually develops in the first few weeks after birth while the ear canal is still closed, usually results from the degeneration of part of the blood supply to the cochlea (the stria vascularis). The nerve cells of the cochlea subsequently die, and permanent deafness results. The cause of the vascular degeneration is not known but appears to be associated with the absence of pigment producing cells (melanocytes) in the blood vessels. In the Dalmatian, where the incidence is highest, 8 percent of all dogs in the U.S. are bilaterally deaf and 22 percent are unilaterally deaf."

As you can see, Dr. Strain's studies on coat color and deafness in dogs mentions the piebald gene, which can create mostly white dogs like Dalmatians.

An article by Caroline Coile from the website "Dogster" further demonstrates how these genetics touch our basic dog-parent worlds, whether we understand them or not. She states, "The merle (also called dapple) pattern is the pattern in which random splotches of dark pigment are overlaid over a lighter shade of the same color. Merle—that kaleidoscope of swirly patterns that has no two dogs looking alike. It's one of the most beautiful coat patterns in the dog world. But merle is definitely a case where too much of a good thing is, well, a bad thing." She goes on to explain the science behind the math and the math behind the popularity.

"Merles are popular, so it seems only logical to breed two merles together to get more merles. No. Don't do it. Here's why: The merle pattern is produced when a dog has a single copy of the M allele. All merle dogs have the genotype *Mm*—meaning they have one allele for merle and one allele for non-merle. All non-merles are *mm*. If you breed a merle (*Mm*) to a non-merle (*mm*) you will, on average, produce a litter in which half of the puppies get the M allele and so are *Mm* (merle) and half get the non-merle allele and so are *mm*. But if you breed two merles together (*Mm* X *Mm*) you will produce, on average, a quarter *mm* (non-merle), a half *Mm* (merle) and a quarter *MM* (double-merle; also called double-dapple). And double merles don't look like merles. Instead, they're mostly white with merle patches. But the main reason you want to avoid producing *MM* dogs is that they often have visual and auditory problems."

Are you confused yet? I am. Even if you have a scientific background and you embrace all these genetics formulas, remember this. Coile goes on to allow this caveat: "Just because a dog is double-merle, don't assume he's deaf."

Sounds simple, right? Just don't breed a merle to a merle or a deaf piebald to another, stand on one foot, hop three times, cross your fingers, so on and so on. Yet the problem of dogs being born deaf still persists. I can give the age-old lecture about reputable breeders, but even that is not enough. There are just too many factors involved, and deafness in the dog world is a matter of fact.

So what should breeders do when deafness crops up? The most conservative approach, of course, would be to not breed the affected animal and not repeat the breeding that produced deafness. It is still frequently recommended by the AKC and the Dalmatian Club of America that bilaterally deaf puppies should be euthanatized; the theory is that they make poor pets, are difficult to train, are prone to startle-biting, frequently die from misadventure (cars), and require excessive care. There is considerable controversy on this point, and there is no question that many people have successfully raised deaf dogs. For every story of a problem deaf dog, there seems to be a story of one that was successfully raised. Unfortunately, there is no way to predict how a deaf puppy will turn out. There are just too many unknown factors that contribute to the problem.

## Vinnie Comes Home

The drive to pick up our new family member was filled with giddy nervousness. What had we done? Would we be a good family for him? Where the heck should we begin? It had been a long time since we'd had a baby in the house, let alone one that couldn't hear. We were nervous but extremely excited.

We prepared as best as we could. We puppy-proofed the house. We got him a puppy collar and leash—all the things you need for a new puppy. We made sure we added a tag with his name on it and a medical warning that he was deaf. If he got away from us, it would be important that anyone unfamiliar knew that they needed to communicate differently with him.

Vinnie was the last puppy to leave the litter, but he was perfectly happy to jump right in the car for a new adventure, no nervousness on his part. Even as an eight-week-old pup, he had no fear. He was not quite as happy to experience the collar and leash, though. They definitely put a damper on his independence and enthusiasm, and he instantly went into "hold me" mode, which my daughter was more than happy to accommodate. This would not be the last time we saw this Academy Award-winning drama.

Vinnie acted like a normal puppy. I am not really sure what we thought he would act like, but *normal* just seemed strange for a special needs dog. He ran and played, he was alert and barked. He came when he was called. My husband, who was the most unsure about our decision, became Vinnie's favorite toy. They played and played, did yard work together, and took late afternoon naps. He just could not believe that the dog could not hear. Vinnie was a normal puppy.

If one of us walked into the house, Vinnie would come running to greet us. If dinner met his dish, he was there in an instant. He must have heard us. How would he know these things? Of course, we did the silly testing things, too—clapping behind him, loud clanging of pans. We even tried a dog whistle. We were sure that the hearing test must have been wrong, but it wasn't wrong.

Eventually, we began noticing how Vinnie watched us ever so intently, how he nervously ran from room to room when waking from a nap until he laid eyes on one of us. When we called him, we hadn't noticed that we unconsciously made hand gestures at the same time. We talked to him like we would have talked to any dog. It didn't matter if he could hear or not, it was impossible not to. Reading some of the training manuals that we found, it was actually a good thing that we did that. Deaf dogs have the uncanny ability to be able to lip read, so to speak. They watch everything, so the natural change in your facial features as you speak is very telling to them. When you are mad, your face changes into an aggressive expression. When you are happy, you smile, and your face is softer. Dogs recognize that. So, with the normal body language we used as we talked to him in conjunction with hand signals that we both were learning, we were communicating fairly well. He was hearing us but not with his ears.

Vinnie would not settle at night in his crate because he could not see us. Once we moved it so he could see us, he was better.

Okay . . . I am totally lying with that statement. We broke the rules and let him into our bed. I know it was not a good thing, but remember, I was just a normal dog mom who melted with one look from those sad, chocolate drop brown eyes. I did start out with the best intentions of using the crate at night; it just didn't last very long. Vinnie's favorite place to sleep was at the foot of the bed, completely under the covers. He had to be touching his people—whoever got the nod for the nap or the night. That was the only way he could finally close those beautiful eyes and relax into a deep, restful slumber.

Vinnie's favorite places to sleep were under the covers in bed or under the coverlet on the chair. He needed to be touching us, but most of all, he needed the solace of no distractions. He was so active that it was the only way he could shut down to truly rest. I believe he felt that if he couldn't see you, you couldn't see him.

Let the training begin.

## Who Trained Whom?

We followed all the tips and directions we had found for both hearing and non-hearing dogs. We printed out hand signal pictures and developed a few of our own. Our research produced standard hand signals, but we found that some of our own seemed to work better. Even the professionals will tell you that's fine, as long as you and the entire family and caregivers use the same ones. Consistency is the name of the game with training any dog, especially a deaf one.

Vinnie responded very well to our communication. We had this. Everything was going well, and then there came the "no closed doors" clause.

If you closed the door to take a shower—or to do any other form of private activities—the dog would literally throw his entire weight behind, pushing the door open, or he would simply have a barking, scratching hissy fit on the other side until that closed door was left open.

I laughed until I cried one morning, watching my husband and Vinnie battling over the bathroom door. My husband wanted to take a shower and absentmindedly closed the door but didn't latch it. Vinnie went flying off the bed and flung the door open wide. Astonished, my husband gave him the wave off and closed the door again. Rinse and repeat, open the door, over and over! I am quite sure I need not describe who won that battle.

We all learned quickly that there would be no more closed doors in Vinnie's life. *No closed doors*! Say it with the same inflection as that famous movie line: "No wire hangers!" Vinnie didn't need to *be* in the room; he just needed to see into the room. He watched everything. Vinnie heard with his eyes, and closed doors just would not do. We attempted to train him, to desensitize him to closed doors, but to no avail. He was willing to learn many things, but this was nonnegotiable. Instead, we learned *we* were trainable. No closed doors.

Potty-training was the next big hurdle that did not go well. Of course, before Vinnie came home with us, we brushed up on all the appropriate training rules for puppies. Always take them to the same door, keep a watchful eye on them constantly, and when they begin walking with stiff legs, run them outside. Keep them focused and praise, praise, praise. We followed all those suggestions. We took him outside repeatedly, and he went to the bathroom appropriately. We praised him, but the next time he needed to go, he went in the house. It just was not working. He was not getting it at all.

I am an avid reader and a computer person—which is one of the biggest reasons I am writing my stories now. I researched Vinnie's potty problems online. I went to bookstores. I contacted dog trainers, browsed through blog sites, and tried anything I could find about working with deaf dogs. There was some good material but not much. I consulted a couple books from dog trainers with intensive workout sessions and high-level functioning, as well as some one-off articles about specific issues, but we were not there yet. The trainers I spoke to admitted that they had no experience with deaf dogs but would be happy to give it a try. How hard could it be?

I told you, you would hear that statement many times.

Most of the material instructed the use of hand signals, how to wake the animal so as not to startle them into biting, and other recommendations like that. That general information was helpful, but we were already working on those things with some good progress. Thus far, no resources hit on the basics we were missing—that "go potty outside" thing. What was wrong? What were we doing wrong?

I had been following a deaf dog blog site ever since I'd learned I would be living with a deaf dog. There was an abundance of good information from caring, thoughtful people who dedicated their time and love to these dogs. It was interesting and confusing all at once. People from all over posted successes and losses; it was like one big, world-spanning family. A great deal of the attention was paid to rescuing deaf dogs who had found themselves abandoned in a shelter. This group did amazing things to try to rescue as many of these dogs as possible. It was fascinating reading. My heart broke for these dogs, and I cheered their successes. But, at the end of the day, I just needed to know how to get one very stubborn puppy to go to the potty outside.

I finally built up the courage to post my question regarding potty-training, and I waited to read the words of wisdom of those deaf-dog parents who had been doing it for far longer than me. With the site's focus on saving so many abandoned dogs, my plight seemed small by comparison. There were a couple of rudimentary suggestions—things we had already tried repeatedly, like "use the same door each time," and "watch them closely" for the signs that it is time, then run them outside.

I had almost given up when I received a note from a lady in Australia. We exchanged private email addresses, and she explained things to me in a way I had not considered before. The lack of hearing in a deaf dog meant that other senses would be heightened to compensate for that missing piece of his perception. That was why Vinnie watched us so intently, would not allow closed doors, smelled us almost before we walked through the door, and did all the other things that had almost convinced us that he could actually hear us.

My new online friend taught me that we had to learn to work to cultivate those things. Most of all, she explained, in the deaf-dog world, *everything* needed to be a routine. Everything needed an action to obtain a reaction. A hand signal meant to do some function, and Vinnie was indeed learning hand signals quickly. We did the hand signal; he did the activity. The missing piece, asking to go out, was not ours to do. It was his. He did not know how to ask to go out. I'd never thought of that. This would be the beginning of thinking differently about basic things.

We hung a bell on the doorknob of the very door we had been using to take him outside. Each time we went out this door, we took his little paw and gave that bell a swipe. I had read before that this was a standard training trick for hearing dogs, but I had never given it a thought as a technique for training a deaf dog, since a deaf dog could not hear a bell. Vinnie could not hear the bell, but we could. He had a function to do that he now understood meant he got to go outside, and I could hear when he needed to go. It was such a simple concept. Potty training . . . Check!

There was some "small print" on the bell-ringing stuff. Bell-ringing also meant squirrel hunting, leaf chasing, or that Dad might be coming home from work soon. It meant he needed to go outside immediately. When the bell rang, we ran.

Routine was another critical component to our training. Vinnie needed routine; he thrived on it. He had his schedule and did well as long as we never deviated too far from that schedule. We all fit our lives around his routine. It did not take a village, but it did take the entire family. Our daughter managed to adjust her college class schedule, my husband and I our work schedules, and Gramma filled in when needed so that Vinnie always had someone with him.

None of us did without or had to give up anything that we wanted to do. We just needed to think differently about how and when we did things. We were very creative. Before long, it was just our norm. We were Vinnie's pack!

## Testing Boundaries

As Vinnie grew, so did his desire to test boundaries. Dalmatians love to run, and they need the space to do so.

We live in the country on four acres. As a pup, Vinnie was content to stay with us and just be a part of what we were doing at the time, but as he grew, so did his desire to see more and go farther. We had a decision to make. He needed space. We could not call him if he strayed too far, like we would a hearing dog. Realistically, we could not fence in the entire yard, and the layout of our property really did not lend well to a fence while providing adequate room for him to run. We also did not want him living his outdoor time on a leash or chain.

We decided we needed an invisible fence. It was a good way to allow Vinnie to run and still contain him safely. We designated part of the yard that we felt gave a good space for activity but still kept him away from any trouble that he might likely get into. We settled on approximately three of the four acres as open space for Vinnie to run around the house. The problem we discovered was that most fences were designed to beep a warning to the dog, then offer a shock if they progressed past their designated boundary. That concept was not going to work. It wasn't fair that he would get no warning, so back to the research we went.

There are indeed fences that offer a beeping warning and a vibration warning at the same time, prior to giving the zap. After calling a few invisible fence dealers and looking at the quotes we received, we felt totally deflated. The cost was astronomical to fence in that much space. The sales pitches stated, "Isn't it worth it to give our dog the best?" Well, yes, but not at the cost of having to sell my soul to afford it! We kept looking.

I firmly believe if you are willing to look long and hard enough, you will find what you need. We did just that. As it turned out, one of the local Farm and Home Coops had a very similar fence that both beeped and vibrated. You could lay out the design you wanted and add additional space as you wished. It was very affordable, but it was going to be a family do-it-yourself project.

On a sunny Saturday afternoon, we rented a trencher and laid out the underground cable. We developed a tag team method. My husband trenched, I followed behind him with the cable and placed it in the hole, my daughter came along behind me and covered the hole with the dirt and put in the interval line markers, and Vinnie followed behind her and dug it all back up and ran off with the flags.

We were all so focused on our tasks at hand that we did not notice the extra help we were receiving for a while. We knew Vinnie was staying close to us; he was busy playing with his shadow, so we were not worried about his safety. We just didn't know yet how sneaky he could be. When we finally turned and noticed what he had done—and saw the yellow cable lying back on top of the ground and Vinnie with a flag in his mouth and a smile on his face—we had no words. He was helping us. We looked at each other, had a good laugh, and began again. He was definitely clever, and he had gotten us. Needless to say, to his dismay, Vinnie got to help with the rest of the project on a leash.

This was just an early chapter of what would become a very long tale of Vinnie-isms. No one could really get mad at or stay mad at Vinnie. He was just a happy guy who enjoyed everything so much. Everything on this planet was put here for his enjoyment, and enjoy things, he did.

The invisible fence was a success. It took us four days of hard labor on our hands and knees around three acres, plus a case of Bengay, but we did it. I am not sure any of us could completely straighten up for about a week, but Vinnie had three acres to run. We read the training directions, and we agreed that each of us had to take a turn walking the perimeter with him so he fully understood that this was his yard and he had to stay within it, and if he chose not to, there would be consequences. Vinnie liked to tattle when he was not able to get his way, so we were a united front. We strategically walked the line for days. Vinnie was not overly interested in this activity, since he felt, "Why walk when you could run?" The directions said if the dog was not paying attention, then it was recommended to give them a shock. Sounds cruel, huh? My daughter and I thought so, too. My husband explained that the setting was on the lowest possible level. We all agreed we would each test it to see. It was no more than a quick rubber band snap.

I will be honest; I am sure my neighbors thought we were all a bit crazy that weekend. My husband and Vinnie investigated this new setting on his collar. Vinnie was not fond of the first couple trips around, but we knew it didn't really hurt him. He quickly responded to the boundary and the exercise. Before we knew it Vinnie had the run of his new yard and stayed within it—or so we thought.

Even with the fence in place, we were still careful. We went outside with Vinnie to be sure that it safely contained him in his respective yard. That was when we discovered that Vinnie had developed a new game.

If he started at the house and had a full head of steam, he could run fast enough across the boundary so that it didn't hurt much. At that point, we had a much clearer appreciation for why there were multiple settings of sensitivity and shock levels. Vinnie got to walk the perimeter again on the leash with a new setting and finally decided he would like to stay inside that perimeter.

In the spring, the Canadian geese love to frequent our yard. We knew the fence was working well when we watched what would be one of the funniest Vinnie moments of all. The geese would purposefully walk just outside of Vinnie's reach to taunt him. Vinnie patiently sat and watched them walk by. We watched him carefully stretch out a leg over the line, then a bit more of his body into almost a Twister-like position. He was testing just how far he could stretch before he felt that telltale vibration. He tried a few more positions, then finally gave up and watched the geese go by. Eventually, he just didn't care, but every once in a while, some goose strayed too close and got a flying lesson.

One thing to remember: an invisible fence is great to keep your wildlife in, but it does nothing to keep nature's wildlife out. To add to our list of Vinnie encounters, his enthusiastic playfulness was on the receiving end of a skunk that was not as keen to play as he was. Vinnie got a face full of skunk spray, then dashed into the house and had wiped it on my family room carpet before anyone had realized he had been sprayed. Unfortunately, my research on cleaning that mess up was not nearly as successful as others. Bath time was not Vinnie's favorite time of day, but he was hard-pressed to gain sympathy from any family member that day. He got to enjoy many baths for several days running. Of course, he was extremely helpful with the relentless rug shampooing as well. With all our fun with this project, it is important to establish that no skunks were harmed in making of this story.

Most dogs eventually wean off the collar once they learn the boundary. Not so with Vinnie. He knew the boundary all right, but he also was smart enough to know that when the collar was not on, the boundary didn't matter. Vinnie got to wear his collar each time he went outside.

# Bad Dogs

Since my family and I have been a part of a Dalmatian's life for over seventeen years—notice, I say we have been a part of *their* lives—we have come to refer to Dalmatians as "bad dogs." They are not really bad dogs, of course. I use the term affectionately, and I am sure several other breeds can boast this same title. They are just so handy and smart that they can get themselves into trouble in the blink of an eye. It is like having a toddler in the house.

I know Dals and some other larger-breed dogs stay in the puppy mindset long after their bodies say otherwise. Vinnie was definitely one of those. He had two speeds: on and off. Everything was one hundred miles an hour. He did well with his hand signals and the basics we worked on with him, but at six months old, it was time for some obedience training. Vinnie needed some manners.

I called several established obedience class groups. Believe it or not, some did not want a deaf dog in their classes. Their reasoning was that they did not trust the behavior of the dog and would not risk others to allow their participation. I attempted to explain that the dog did not have a contagious disease and that he was doing well with the training we were working on. They wanted no part of it. Others openly admitted they had never worked with a deaf dog. They were willing to try but could not guarantee any results.

Should I say it? How hard could it be, right?

We did find a group that was willing to give us a try. They also revealed that they had some experience with deaf dogs but not a lot. They would treat him like a hearing dog until they could not. That sounded like a good plan.

Vinnie did exceptionally well at class. He sat, and everyone marveled at his eye contact and how well he behaved. Of course, I did not admit that aliens must have switched my dog with this one, because he certainly never acted this well-behaved at home.

When everyone else was using voice commands, I was using hand signals. Thanks to his diligent eye contact, he did not notice the chaos around us. And there was one big advantage he had over the others. Sound disruptions did not bother him a bit. We completed a nine-week class, and he graduated on the honor roll. I won't venture so far as to say that Vinnie had developed many manners, but he would sit and lie down on command. He would stay if he felt like it and there was food involved, and he walked nicely on a leash. He socialized well with the people and their pets there.

The directors of the group had given us a few names to try for further training and the contact information of others in the area who were living with deaf dogs. With my newfound confidence that a deaf dog could really live a normal hearing dog life with a few tools, I was excited to finally speak with others like me.

We met with a trainer who'd had success at training deaf dogs. She came to our home and met with my family and Vinnie, and she was very impressed with the high level of functionality Vinnie had developed under our guidance. She suggested the use of a laser pointer to get his attention when he was having difficulty with distractions or when he was outside away from eye contact. She also suggested ways that we could afford him some more independence but still be able to get his attention.

Unfortunately, a laser pointer was never going to work as a training tool. We had discovered, when he was a pup. that he loved chasing the cat's laser pointer. It was great fun. As a result, it was a toy. At the time, we had no idea of the ramifications. That was a mistake on our part, but luckily, we were able to use other techniques to get his attention—which usually consisted of erratically flailing our arms about. We looked like crazy people, but he knew what it meant. At night, when he was outside, we could flick the outside light off and on repeatedly, and he knew to come to the house to see what was up. All and all, we were doing okay.

I was given another contact that I decided to reach out to, and I spoke with a woman who was caring for several deaf dogs. She told me many things that I already knew, but she also shared some information that I did not want to hear. She gave me some pretty straight, hard facts about the complications that some dogs experience due to whatever caused their deafness.

Unfortunately, there is never a definitive way to know why a dog is born deaf. The science of genetics I explained earlier is first and foremost, but there are always other contributing factors that play a role. My new friend explained that other neurological issues might also be present or could present themselves at a later time.

Of course, there is the expected response to startling a dog that obviously sleeps soundly due to no noise disruptions, but she said also it was not uncommon for deaf dogs to develop different forms of OCD and sometimes aggression issues. She told me to watch him closely around the one-year mark, which was when hormonal changes might cause the dog to exhibit those types of behaviors. Some dogs had to be euthanized, since there was little that could be done at that point.

She said if the benchmark came and went, we might be okay. She was not an expert; she was a dog mom just like me who loved her dogs. I liked her very much, but I didn't like hearing the hard truth. This was one of my first "head in the sand" moments, and I was a little bit scared. Our Vinnie was doing so well. You couldn't even tell he was deaf unless you knew it. Those things just were not going to happen to us. We were the lucky ones.

# He Loves Me, He Loves Me Not

Vinnie loved us, there was no doubt. He loved being a part of anything and everything we did. If we were outside, he wanted to be outside. If we were inside, that was fine too. He was a lucky guy to have found us, and we were a lucky family to have him.

Vinnie took his lead from us and often mimicked us. One day, my husband was sitting in the garage talking with my daughter on her way out. He sat on the hood of the lawn tractor during their conversation. He turned to find Vinnie sitting beside him on the hood of the tractor, like this was what he should be doing.

For the most part, Vinnie's puppy phase went fairly well, and most of his antics brought us a good deal of laughter. Don't get me wrong—Vinnie spent a great deal of time in trouble, because his strategy was usually to ask for forgiveness over asking for permission. Simply being a puppy is as much to blame for that as anything.

Vinnie had a thing for flowers. I call it a "thing" because I am not really sure if he liked them or disliked them. What

I do know is that he loved running through them and ripping off the blooms. Daylilies, hostas—anything that bloomed was susceptible to Vinnie's pruning.

There were a couple of stationary pots in the front of the house that, in the offseason, were not planted with growing foliage. I had used silk arrangements so that the pots were not unsightly and ugly. Leaving the house one day, I noticed them empty. It had been windy the previous night, so I thought they had been blown out. I walked the yard and, sure enough, found them and replaced them.

The next day, the same thing had happened. It took a couple days before I discovered what was going on. It was not the wind after all; it appeared as though even these flowers could not escape the perils of Hurricane Vinnie. As he bounded off the front porch to the yard, he would grab a flower head as he flew by and run away with it. It was a graceful, stealthy move that happened so quickly that it went unnoticed for quite some time. He did not wish to destroy them, just remove them. It was a game.

In the summer, this game was replaced with grabbing the flower pots full of flowers. He was not quite as graceful with this maneuver due to the weight of the planted pot, but it was equally as fun. We worked with Vinnie constantly on these things, but at the same time, they made us smile. He didn't mean to be bad; it just came naturally to him.

None of this was because the poor dog had no toys. Vinnie had many toys, and we played with him constantly. He quickly learned to catch a Frisbee, and he played a terrible game of fetch—he fetched but never wanted to return. He was just full of puppy.

My husband brought him home some special bones on occasion from the butcher. They were the kind that did not splinter or break, could not really be chewed up, and had the yucky marrow still in them. Vinnie would take them and lick and chew for hours, which I think was my husband's secret weapon for getting some things done while he was occupied.

One day, after enjoying a bone for a while, Vinnie went outside with it and disappeared in the yard. When he returned, there was no bone. We never gave it a thought until later, when he kept ringing the bell to go back outside. He had buried his bone prior to being called in, and each time he went back outside, he dug it up and moved it to a new location. This went on through several relocations until I think he finally forgot where he buried it. I understand that dogs competing with other animals bury their things, but Vinnie had no competition. We had a good laugh about it. It was another silly Vinnie thing.

Then, one day, I came home from work, and the family met me at the door. They all wore rather sheepish expressions. My daughter explained that before I came in, I needed to know that Vinnie had been naughty, and I needed to stay calm. I hate those preamble warnings.

I walked into the house and saw what they were nervous about revealing to me. Somehow, Vinnie had snuck one of his bones into the house. He had attempted to bury it in a very large potted plant by digging it up. When that apparently failed, he'd attempted to bury it in the cushions of the sofa, then a chair, and then the middle of my bed. Needless to say, there was a great deal of mud from one end of the house to the other.

I am fairly certain that Vinnie knew he had exceeded the forgiveness marker. He sat still, very quietly watching. I had to laugh; otherwise, I would have cried. It was like scolding a child while trying to maintain a straight face to keep from laughing at their antics. These are the stories we will cherish forever.

## Obsessive Compulsive Disorder

Obsessive Compulsive Disorder (OCD) is diagnosed when a dog repeats activities out of context or does the same activity over and over. OCD is not something every deaf dog experiences. It is not a side effect of deafness; it is a complication.

Many hearing dogs also experience OCD. Some pet trainers feel that the onset of OCD is due to an unbalanced diet. Some feel that it is stress-related. Others feel that it is more breed-related. The Deaf Dog Education Action Fund Website posts that OCD has been documented with higher statistics in active, intelligent breeds such as Dalmatians, Australian Shepherds, Border Collies, and Jack Russell Terriers. OCD can be present in mild to severe cases, and there is no specific treatment for this ailment. Suggestions range from mentally and physically stimulating your dog in healthy ways to being careful not to reward OCD behavior. Extremely severe cases may need to be treated with medication.

Vinnie was a silly guy. He ran, he played, and he chased his tail like many puppies did. His antics of chasing shadows and reflections began as a pup, and we thought they were cute and funny. We did not understand that they were an issue and would continue to manifest and worsen as he aged.

We attempted to redirect him when he was overly focused on a specific thing. We had to draw the curtains or put our cell phones and watches in dark places if the light caught them. Anything that could make a sparkle on the wall or ceiling became a lethal weapon. Vinnie would literally climb the wall to get to them. I have found scratches in the drywall in places that make me wonder how the dog managed to get there. I was quite sure I had never found wings on him. Maybe there was a secret kangaroo relative somewhere in his bloodline.

The habit of chasing his tail waned but was replaced by chewing on his tail instead. He would chew it until it was slimy and wet, usually when he was overtired. He never got to the point of it becoming raw or bloody, but, again, the only option we had was to redirect his behavior. We would give him a toy or throw a ball. We tried anything to get him to focus on a different behavior. Chasing shadows was a complicated process to avoid. If the sun was out, there was a shadow. Any shadow would do. Vinnie would literally knock you off your feet to get to your shadow.

Vinnie seemed like a happy guy, and all this was great fun. We knew he had a good, balanced diet. He had a great disposition, he got a ton of exercise, received plenty of rest and time out when he was overtired, and, from our vantage point, it seemed as though his highest amount of stress came from anticipating his next meal. We came to this conclusion based on his habit of carrying around his bowl when it got close to meal time. He enjoyed reminding you that it was nearly time. After all, Vinnie's favorite time of day was mealtime.

The habit of chewing his tail did get much better, but, unfortunately, it was not always possible to avoid all reflections and shadows, especially if it was a bright, sunny day. I felt that his heightened reliance on sight, due to his deafness, most likely was a big factor with this obsession. We were told to never punish but also never reward OCD behavior—it was something he could not help—but instead to use positive reinforcement training to alter his energies. His OCD never jeopardized his health as far as we could tell; it was just an annoying, obnoxious behavior.

We tried to keep him socialized with other dogs. We arranged play dates with neighbors who had fenced-in yards; dog play is different than people play. He enjoyed that a great deal. We also added a few days of Doggie Day Care to keep him socialized outside of his everyday world and help with positive stimulation. He returned home good and tired, hungry and happy. Unfortunately, reflections and shadows were still impressive to him. It was just something we all learned to live with, and we did what we could to minimize it as much as possible.

# Doggie Day Care

Before Vinnie, I never knew there was such a thing as doggie day care or that it was such a competitive business. When my office moved to a new location in a different town about an hour away, I noticed a very cute place near where we picked up lunch. I peeked in the window and found adorable dogs playing in a doggie jungle gym. I decided to take a tour. The ladies who worked there were very nice and were willing to give my Vinnie a try.

We were excited; it was the like the first day of school for our guy. We packed his backpack with a travel bowl and lunch. Even though Vinnie loved riding in the car, it was quite a distance, so I wanted him to be safe. Vinnie got a seat belt to ensure that he would stay in the back seat—I did not want to run the risk of him trying to drive the car. Knowing his personality, I knew it would only be a matter of time until he did. So, off to day care we went.

I did warn them that he was deaf and a very energetic young man. He did well for the first few days, but it did not take long for him to find some trouble. Vinnie figured out how to open the door and let himself into the grooming area whenever he wanted. He played a little rough for some of the smaller dogs, and he was just far too wild for the owner's taste.

One afternoon, when I walked in to pick Vinnie up, the receptionist's hair was standing on end, her head was in her hands, and I knew almost instantly that Vinnie was the most likely suspect for the cause of her disheveled appearance. I was right; Vinnie had not had a good day. That was the day my boy got kicked out of day care. If it hadn't been so funny, I would probably have been embarrassed.

We found out the hard way that not all doggie day-care centers are created equally. It is easy to open a business, put a sign on your door, and promote your expertise, but this type of business is not for just anyone. This day-care operation was simply a groomer who had some space and earned some extra money by babysitting dogs. They were not really prepared to handle what we brought them. To their defense, they did not understand how to work with high-energy dogs, nor did they fully appreciate the special needs of a deaf dog. They were not equipped to handle him.

I had a clearer view of their lack of knowledge when I picked Vinnie up one day, and they were alarmed that the hair stylist from the shop next door had come over to tell them that she had witnessed me trying to beat my dog in the car that morning. Of course, I hadn't done anything of the sort. It had been a windy day, and the corner of the business plaza had become a wind tunnel. Some trash had been blowing around and around, circling the car. Vinnie, with his proclivity for OCD, had been fascinated and incensed, and I could not get him to calm down.

I had just unhooked his seatbelt, and he was throwing himself against the glass of the car, trying to reach the swirling paper. Concerned that he would injure himself, I tried to get his attention by waving my hands in front of him to get him to focus on me instead of whatever had him out of control. The busybody hairdresser saw my arms moving but did not look any further to see the outcome; she could not see what I was really doing. Once under control, Vinnie entered day care as always. The owner explained to me that the hairdresser was going to call the SPCA to file a report. I was not really surprised at the simplemindedness of the hairdresser, but I was surprised by the lack of support of the day care owner. She had watched me numerous times use similar techniques with Vinnie. I asked her if she had explained this to the lady, and she admitted she had not. She had just stated that the dog was not an abused dog. I do not think she understood well enough to explain, which served to validate why Vinnie was no longer welcome there.

Luckily, the area I worked in boasted two doggie day care facilities. I went in with a humble heart and my head hung low and explained my predicament to the new establishment. Vinnie loved going to day care a couple of days a week, and since my family's schedules had needed to change a bit, we needed some help—not to mention that a tired Vinnie was a much better behaved Vinnie. Notice I did not say a "good" Vinnie. He was my bad dog, and I would not have it any other way!

The owner of the second day-care center smiled, took me by the hand, and gave me the full tour. He introduced me to this dog and that dog and the other dog, all of whom had *also* been kicked out of the other day-care center. They were not ill-behaved dogs, just high-energy dogs that the first day-care center did not have the skill set to handle. All of them were thriving at this new place. It was a beautiful, family-run facility and was laid out much nicer with different rooms for dogs of different sizes and energy levels. I was both impressed and thrilled with this amazing place, and I could not wait for Vinnie to give it a try.

I explained that Vinnie was deaf and that we had a page of hand signals. That did not fuss them at all. They even met Vinnie when I brought him in a few days later with all the appropriate signals already learned. They had no problem accommodating Vinnie's schedule. He needed to eat lunch and have some quiet time around midday so he didn't get overtired. At this place, the dogs came first.

As it turned out, the first facility had done us a huge favor by kicking us out. On the days when Vinnie went to his new day care, he proudly rode in the car with his seatbelt on. It kept his hind end in the back seat, but he sat patiently watching out the window of the car, waiting to play with his friends. When we were a couple of miles away, he would start to get very excited. I am not sure exactly how he knew where we were, to be truthful. The only explanation I have is that Vinnie's sight was so good that he had learned to gauge his location by the familiar sites as we passed. It was impressive that he seemed to know where he was, as he almost always reacted at the same location, about five minutes away from our destination. Vinnie loved going there.

He seemed always to have a smile on his face on those days. At the end of the day, he walked to the car at a much slower pace than his usual "let me in there" cadence in the mornings. We would receive a full report of "Vinnie-isms" when we picked him up. All were filled with much laughter. He was a funny guy, and they kept their sense of humor because they were prepared to handle him. It was a good fit for all of us!

They welcomed us like we were family, and they became like family to us, as well. They knew each dog by name and cared deeply for them. Vinnie might never have experienced this wonderful place if the first facility hadn't kicked him out. The most important thing of all was that we landed in a place that focused on the dogs and their families.

# Vinnie Language!

**SIT**

**GOOD**

**STAY**

**DOWN**

**COME**

**HERE**

**NO**

It is better to talk to Vinnie even though he cannot hear. Your facial expressions are more accurate when you speak the words!

## Oh My!

We quickly learned that Vinnie's expressions and mannerisms were almost human. We never needed to wonder what the dog wanted. As I mentioned earlier, absolutely everything was put on this planet for his entertainment; so, needless to say, he was one happy guy most of the time.

When things were wrong, though, they were really, really wrong. When Vinnie did not feel well, you could tell immediately. As with any puppy, tummy aches and pains happen, so you carefully observe and follow the usual puppy procedures, and most clear up in a day or so.

Around the six-month mark, Vinnie stopped eating one day. This was extremely unusual behavior for him, since Vinnie's favorite time of day was meal time. He was not vomiting or showing signs of sickness, just not eating. We kept a close eye on him and offered the food at his usual meal times. He smelled it and walked away. He was not even interested in his treats. We watched and waited. After a day of not eating, we offered the bland rice diet. Still, it was a no-go, and when he stopped drinking, we called the vet.

Dehydration is a dangerous thing for a dog and can take hold very quickly, causing catastrophic results. It seemed that Vinnie went from not acting sick at all one day to being very sick the next. He wanted to be held constantly and was shaking. Shaking is an unmistakable sign that the dog is in discomfort. The changes in his condition happened later that evening, which precipitated our decision not to wait to see his usual vet the next day; we rushed him to the Emergency Care Facility. Little did we know then, that decision most likely saved his life and would change our lives from that point on.

This emergency visit was our first experience with the animal ER system. At first glance, it seemed a bit impersonal. They gave us the cost of walking in the door before we even entered the facility. Mind you, the cost was significant, but when it is your beloved pet, it just does not matter. Vinnie was hurting.

The folks at the facility were kind to us and comforting to Vinnie. They explained that they needed to sedate him to calm him and help him with his discomfort and to do a series of X-rays to see what was going on. His symptoms suggested that he had a blockage in his intestines. We patiently waited for the results of the tests.

His results showed that we had made the right decision by not waiting to see the vet the following day. He was becoming badly dehydrated very quickly. He was placed on an IV to correct that. He responded well and seemed much more comfortable almost immediately. Then we received the bad news from the X-rays. Vinnie did indeed have a blockage in his intestines. It was unclear exactly what it was, but what was clear was that it was not good. The blockage needed to be removed immediately to save the dog.

Again, the estimate paper was produced. Again, the cost was significant. Again, the decision was clear. Vinnie was a member of our family and he needed help. Off to surgery!

The following morning, Vinnie's prognosis was good. He did well in surgery and would survive. He sported a rather long wound on his belly and an unwelcome Elizabethan collar. We met with the vet and were presented with his trophy of shame. The contents of his blockage were neatly tucked in a plastic bag to show us.

Upon first glance of the contents of that bag, my daughter burst into tears. She was almost inconsolable. She sobbed, saying that she almost killed Vinnie. After getting her calmed down, we learned the story of Vinnie's misfortune.

That ziplocked bag held a very small ball of plastic wrap—just a small piece of Saran Wrap from a sandwich. My daughter lamented that a couple days previously, she had unwrapped her sandwich, and on her the way to the garbage can, Vinnie had snatched it out of her hand. Her account of the situation was simple; he had slurped it down before she could even react to get it away from him. She had not felt it was relevant, since it was just a tiny piece of wrap.

We learned a great deal that day. That very small piece of wrap had balled up, become petrified, and actually perforated Vinnie's intestines. He would have died, had we not been receptive to his discomfort.

The vet agreed with our daughter, that she, too, would not have taken the situation very seriously. The plastic wrap tasted like food, and that was why he'd grabbed it and eaten it. Animals often easily pass the silly things they eat in a few days, and the plastic wrap was not very big. That was just not the case this time. Though the vet's words did little to make our daughter feel better, it was definitely a learning experience for all of us, since it was our first encounter with foreign object ingestion. Sadly, it would not be our last.

Vinnie recovered very quickly, and within a day or so, he was back to his usual, silly self. He fussed with the cone but readily ate the bland diet at every meal. Mealtime was back, regardless of what it consisted of. His wound healed quickly and was barely visible. We were back to normal—if that is what you would call our lives with Vinnie.

Kelly Artieri

## Pica – Huh?

Foreign object ingestion is, unfortunately, very common with dogs, especially puppies. Puppies are in constant motion, and part of the way they investigate their new world is to put things in their mouths. Nothing wrong with eating a bit of dirt, a stick or two, and, of course, the occasional pebble is always on the menu. For puppies, everything is fair game, especially when it tastes like a sandwich, as in Vinnie's case. Remember, what constitutes acceptable food to us differs greatly to dogs and is still considered acceptable behavior. Investigative behavior is normal, but it becomes a problem when it advances to eating things that should not be eaten on a regular basis. It becomes an affliction known as Pica.

The basic, clinical definition of Pica, from PetMD Online Medical Encyclopedia, is "the craving and compulsive eating of nonfood substances." This disease can affect both humans and animals.

Your vet will help determine if this random eating disorder is being precipitated by a real medical problem due to illness. Once those areas have been dispelled, behavior must be looked at. Boredom and anxiety can be culprits, as can stress and frustration from conflict. It can be an attention-grabbing concept or a power play to show dominance, and, of course, OCD behaviors always influence behavior disorders.

Pica? What the heck? Huh?

The Humane Society of the United States takes the stand that while theories on this disorder are often proven and disproven just as quickly, no firm reason has been pinpointed as the cause. They recommend that it is a good idea to seek the help of an animal behavior specialist as well as a veterinarian. Pica prevention becomes a training process for your pet as well as your family, depending on the type of Pica your pet suffers from. My favorite quote is from dog trainer Jolanta Benal: "An ounce of prevention is worth a dozen emergency gastric surgeries." Little did we know just how true that quote was.

Depending on the source you may read, you will find many different opinions on why this disease occurs. It can range from possible missing dietary nutrients to mental illness, from aggression disorders to inferiority complexes. In other words, no one really knows, but everyone has an idea. In humans, you can offer psychiatric help. With animals, you might need to seek psychiatric help for yourself by the time you are done.

All kidding aside, it is a very serious illness that requires constant supervision. We did not understand the true meaning of the term at the time. It was just a piece of plastic wrap that tasted like the sandwich it had contained. We had control of this. The surgery had gone well, and Vinnie was fine. It was just another chapter in the story of Vinnie and my family. After all, how hard can it be when you love them lots?

## Round Two

I believe it was not quite six months after our first encounter with the ingestion of a foreign object—the notorious plastic wrap—when it happened again. Vinnie was playing with his stuffed dolphin toy, a toy he had played with since coming to live with us almost a year prior. One evening, for some reason, he decided to pull all the stuffing from it, and then it disappeared.

We panicked. We searched high and low, looking for the carcass, praying that it was just absentmindedly discarded instead of what we all feared, that it had been eaten! It was nowhere to be found.

We looked up the emergency procedure for ingestion of a foreign object when it was immediately noticed. We were instructed to administer hydrogen peroxide in intervals based on the dog's weight. This was supposed to allow the dog to vomit the contents of his stomach to keep the object from going any further into the gastric system.

After several tries, it didn't work. Nothing came up. We did not know for sure if he had eaten it, and we were hopeful that he had nothing to throw up, which was why nothing was coming up. That wish soon proved in vain when Vinnie again began to exhibit those telltale signs that he had eaten something bad. Of course, it was during a time when his normal vet was not available, so off to the emergency clinic we went again. We chose a different location this time, closer to home, due to the time and proximity, but the process was eerily similar.

I kept a binder with all Vinnie's medical history and vet visits. It came in handy more than once, since it seemed he never got sick during normal business hours. I explained in detail Vinnie's previous surgery and what led up to it, and I provided copies of the X-rays and medical reports from his normal vet and the past ER veterinarian.

Again, we were advised to admit, sedate, and X-ray Vinnie. And yes, it was accompanied with a hefty price quote. Well, we loved him lots, so off he went. The results were obvious. There on the X-ray was the shape of a small dolphin in his intestines. It needed to be surgically removed. We knew that.

This was the point when we could no longer deny that Pica had officially entered our lives. It was the beginning of many changes for everyone in Vinnie's life!

# Complications

Vinnie survived his "dolphin-ectomy." After a few days in the hospital, he came home, but this time, it was different.

He didn't bounce back the way he had before. The incision looked the same, but Vinnie would not eat, was barely drinking, and his belly was very swollen. He was lethargic and listless. We went back to the current treating vet multiple times and were given the same response: "Your dog just underwent a very serious surgery, and it takes time to recuperate. Let's wait and see."

We have all been told to trust in our medical professionals, but as parents and pet parents, we know when things are just not right. Things were not right! Vinnie's belly got bigger and bigger, and you could hear liquid sloshing about when he walked. I know I am not a medical professional—I just played one on TV—but something was not right.

At this point, we had been back to the vet several times, only to be told to just wait and see and let him heal. Mind you, this was not my normal vet; this was the vet who had operated on him, so I felt it necessary to complete the process with them. After all, I had paid a great deal of money, and they held the records, as well as having held his intestines. They should know, right? Not to mention, they made me feel as if I were overreacting and just needed to "wait and see."

I took time off of work and stayed with Vinnie around the clock. He was a sick boy. Finally, a few days after his surgery, of not eating, and of feeling terrible, he threw up, and so many questions were answered.

There it was in a pile of vomit. There was the answer to him not getting any better: about a foot and a half of gauze, a small, plastic wheel, a catheter, and some random pieces of white plastic material. Even in my shock, I managed to secure the entire mess into a gallon-size ziplock bag. I then gathered my Vinnie up and we went back to the vet's office.

When I produced the bag with its contents—along with my dismay—they very quickly escorted us to a private examination room. I politely and professionally asked them if there was something that they had forgotten to mention to me. In most things, the story all comes out eventually.

As it went, it appeared that Mr. Vinnie and his Pica struck again. While sedated, in a cage, with a cone on, and under supervision, he had managed to eat the cone, the IV catheter, and his gauze and had possibly managed to give himself another blockage—all while under supervision at the hospital after surgery.

As I explained my disbelief and disappointment, I was met with blank stares from the vet, along with the curt reminder that my dog had an eating disorder. *Hello!* We all knew that when he came in!

Vinnie would need to be sedated and X-rayed again and they would be happy to supply me with yet another price quote, even though this time it had happened on their watch! What choice did we have at that juncture? I paid the bill, the X-rays were done, and the vet showed me the area of concern. It did not show a blockage per se, but it was a semi-opaque area that was not normal. She admitted that she did not know what it was. We would need to wait and see.

I will admit, I lost that little filter between my brain and my mouth at that moment.

After my head finished spinning completely around, I very sincerely but bluntly asked them how they could even look me in the face and charge me for fixing an issue that had happened under their supervision while the dog was in their care. I had told them that he had an eating disorder when I'd brought him in. They had surgically removed the previous results of his eating disaster, so none of that information was anything new to them. It was obvious to me that the dog had not been sedated properly, the cone had not been installed properly, or he had not been supervised or checked as often as I was told he would be.

I have to say the words again to impress my frustration: He was a sedated puppy in a cage with a cone on, who was supposed have been checked at specific intervals! All the repeat trips while the dog was failing to thrive were accompanied by a charge, and never once did they feel the need to admit what had happened. They must have known what the culprit was. If he had not thrown up the evidence, we might never have known. Were they just going to allow the dog to continue to fail?

These were all good questions that were also met with blank stares. "Let's wait and see!"

As I recount this story, I am still shaking my head that they not only never admitted what had happened until I took a bag of vomit in to confront them, but that they felt they had no obligation of accountability whatsoever. The worst part, to me, was that they were allowing the dog to suffer instead of owning the responsibility! Vinnie was dying, and they knew it!

Vinnie and I took that opportunity to walk out of the office as fast as our wobbly legs could carry us. I am a strong but softhearted parent, as most are. You can kick me, punch my husband, we can defend ourselves, but you darn well better not even look cross-eyed at my kid or my pets!

Vinnie was so sick, and I thought I had done the right things. I called my normal vet, apologized profusely for dragging in someone else's mess for her to fix, and drove straight there. She took one look at him, handed me a tissue, and commented that she was horrified that another professional could have left the dog in that condition. Then I produced the bag of goodies. I almost needed to hand *her* the tissue at that point. She, like me, was astonished at the negligence she was witnessing from medical professionals in her field.

I produced the X-rays that the previous vet—who had not known what to make of them—and instantly, my vet knew what was wrong. It was ascites, an accumulation of fluid in the abdomen due to complications of the surgery he had undergone a few days prior. Something internally was leaking fluid into his abdomen at an alarming rate. That fluid was what was causing his abdomen to be so bloated and the sloshing sound when he moved.

By this time, the fluid had gotten so bad with the "let's wait and see" prognosis that the dog was beginning to have difficulty breathing and had a raging fever from the fluid becoming infected in his belly. Vinnie was very sick and was admitted so that the fluid could be addressed immediately.

Several liters of fluid were drawn from Vinnie's abdomen and sent out for diagnostic testing. My vet suspected that something had either been damaged during surgery or that the medical waste he had ingested had caused damage on its way in or out.

I have always found it fascinating what medical professionals can tell from lab results. The independent lab results showed that his bile duct was damaged, as was his pancreas. The report indicated that both problems were, most likely, the result of possible rough handling during surgery. The medical waste was also not ruled out as a complicating factor. Regardless, it was suggested that the fluid be removed. IV antibiotics needed to be administered, IV hydration was imperative, and the dog was to be put on a bland diet and watched very closely for any other complications.

The fluid needed to be drawn a few times, but with the correct medical care, Vinnie became Vinnie again. The rest of us, however, would never be the same.

Not only did we need to care for him post-surgery, but we had to take affirmative action on the Pica front. We no longer could excuse our previous version of what had happened. The plastic wrap may have tasted like a sandwich, but catheters, Elizabethan cones, and medical gauze did not. We had no idea what randomly caused him to eat a toy he had been playing with for months without incident. We needed to do some serious research and find some professional help.

We had Pica! Our family now had an eating disorder!

# Nothing Smaller Than a Beach Towel

How many times have pet parents wished they knew what went on in the brains of their pets? For us, that was the understatement of the year.

As what had happened began coming into clearer focus, other random acts began to surface that we hadn't previously given much thought. I remember noticing missing socks in the laundry, seeing random, unidentifiable objects in the pooper scooper—things that could have just been puppy-related or unrelated entirely. In our case, it was becoming obvious; they were most likely all related. We just didn't realize it at the time.

Not only is Pica not completely understood, but factor in the quick onset and randomness of Vinnie's recent activities, and we had to quickly get very serious about it. I read everything I could get my hands on. Some of it was helpful, some not so much. It became more of the same: making a plan for ourselves.

The most important element in the training of any dog—especially in something like a life or death situation—is consistency and repetition. All family members must be on the same page, and they must exercise appropriate practices religiously. No exceptions could be tolerated!

One of the main components continually mentioned in my reading was the boredom factor. Vinnie was a very active guy and all puppy. We consistently made sure he had a great deal of exercise every day, but he was also a heavy chewer and needed stimulation on top of that. We needed to provide him with toys, or he would make his own. As with any puppy, Vinnie's toy choices would be far different from ours. From now on, we had to be careful about what was safe for him to play with.

Our plan began with removing all plush or small toys that could be torn apart or eaten. They were replaced with large Kong brand dog toys geared for the extreme chewer or Nylabones. We selected a variety of items with different shapes and flavors to provide a variety to help prevent boredom. We were at a disadvantage, since we could not use sound and light to entertain him due to his OCD and deafness. It became a challenge of size, taste, and texture. You would be surprised how much you can find when you look.

We made the process fun. The old toys disappeared when Vinnie was not present, and a new, "safe" toy was left to be found. It was like Christmas morning over and over. We developed new games with these new toys, and before long, the old toys were a thing of the past. It was important that we kept a full inventory of toys at the end of each day and a watchful eye on the condition of each. If one disappeared or began to be worn or chewed to a smaller or fragmented size, it was quickly whisked out of sight and disposed of. The toy was immediately replaced with a new one, and the game continued.

Just like young children seem to select their one, special toy or blanket for comfort, Vinnie had his black ball. He played fetch with it, he chewed on it, he carried it around, and whatever he was feeling at the time was shared with that black ball. The black ball went everywhere—even to bed. We purchased several black balls, so one was easily replaced as quickly as possible when its predecessor became too badly chewed. I believe, in total, Vinnie went through six black balls.

The entire family was a part of our plan, and everyone did their part. It became our new routine. Nothing could be left in coat pockets or purses unzipped. The yard within Vinnie's perimeter needed to be walked daily to remove anything that had been thrown or dropped. Food wrappers and containers could not be left on counters. No socks, undergarments, dishrags, sponges, or clothing could be left anywhere within reach or climbing distance. Our motto became: Nothing smaller than a beach towel could be left down or uncontained.

# Normality?

I have mentioned the word "normal" many times throughout my stories. To be truthful, we were anything but normal, but we were settling in quite nicely to our routines, normal or not. It seemed as though after each catastrophic event, we could again find some piece of normality before we ventured into a new issue with Vinnie—well, *our* normality, anyway.

Vinnie healed and began to thrive again. We stayed true to our new plans, which had to remain dynamic to keep up. We all had our jobs and responsibilities, and we used thorough checks and balance to be sure none of us slipped up. Vinnie was a smart guy, and he worked hard to be a part of our plans. He settled down a bit, mimicked our actions, and kept up his end of the deal.

We went to work; we creatively altered our schedules to be with Vinnie as much as possible. He did well at day care. He stayed inside his invisible fence. We all were doing well. None of it was a sacrifice; it was just what you did when you needed to do it. You create your own normality.

We never stopped investigating and learning. While in our discovery phases, learning about one of his disabilities or another, we spoke with many different organizations about other training options for deaf dogs.

One day, during a break from one of the obedience classes, we watched the agility classes that were offered in the next arena. Vinnie was mesmerized, watching the dogs run through their paces. We were intrigued. Could this be our next plan to work through?

We spoke with the instructor, who was far less enthusiastic than we were about giving it a try. She admitted that Vinnie had done extremely well with basic obedience skills via hand signals, but she felt the agility part would be more difficult to convert, since many of their commands were based on whistles and sounds. Remember, I mentioned before that deaf dogs are barred from participating in sanctioned competitions of any kind.

Recommendations for OCD and Pica refer to keeping the animal happy, well-exercised, and stimulated. A normal Dalmatian is at his happiest when he is active and running. Agility training seemed like a good combination for us to try. We called around, looking for an agility club who would work with us or at least allow us to use their facility to work with Vinnie on our own. To me, it did not seem to be such a stretch to replace sounds and whistles with hand signals. The agility we saw used some hand signals as it was. Possibly, other areas offered this, but we were unable to find a group that wanted to take us on for agility. Sadly, we never quite accomplished that piece of our puzzle. Though not universal yet, there are people who are beginning to look more positively at some agility competitions for hearing-impaired dogs. Today, that remains on my to-do list.

Our first year together seemed like a whirlwind tour of a little bit of anything and everything all thrown together. It seemed like once we leaped over one hurdle, another and another appeared. Vinnie grew from an adorable pup to a handsome young man. His eyes were bright, his coat was shiny, his slim figure was back intact, and his scars were barely visible. Vinnie loved everyone, and everyone loved him.

Year one blurred quickly into year two with many emotions, laughs, and snuggles, but no more tearful emergencies.

Finally . . . normality. True normality!

## The Terrible Twos

Time passed, and we soon celebrated Vinnie's second birthday. Vinnie was still a bad boy on many occasions, but he was an active, healthy dog. Larger-breed dogs and Dalmatians in particular remain mentally in the puppy mindset long after their bodies say otherwise. This was no surprise to us; Spot, our previous Dal, had the same affliction. We had expected Vinnie to get into trouble from time to time, like any dog does—just not life-threatening troubles of his first year.

We had passed all the milestones that we had been cautioned about. We now managed to address the cursory events like bath time, crating, not being too rough with the cat, and all the everyday silliness of happy dog ownership. This was a pleasant change for us.

Bath time was a special time. You would have thought we were throwing the dog into a boiling tar pit, given the way he acted each time a bath was suggested. He managed to survive each one without incident, and, since he was a treat-driven dog, he usually made out rather well in that regard. He also quickly understood that I was not falling for the nonsense. Mom was not a pushover when a bath was needed, especially since he benefitted by being allowed to be in our bed.

We did not crate Vinnie at night. We allowed him to sleep with us, and we all were fine with it. He was clean. He had his space, and we had ours. We all liked our sleep far more than winning the battle of him sleeping in the crate. In fact, our snuggle times together were some of the best times I remember. Vinnie had done well with his crate during the times the family could not arrange to have someone home with him, and we were careful to keep his crate time to a minimum in duration and consistency. It was time for the next phase of his training. Staying home alone was our new challenge.

Knowing that Vinnie had OCD, Pica, and a bit of separation anxiety when he could not lay eyes on us, we were nervous about how to proceed, but our concerns were unfounded. Vinnie grasped the concept and accepted the practice rather easily. We left his crate in place and open as his safe place that he was accustomed to. We limited our absences to realistic times and kept all his routines and schedules in mind. We could not afford to take any chances.

Most of the time, we would come home to find him fast asleep on top of his crate, so we put a comforter on top to make it more comfortable for him. That spot became his favorite vantage point from then on. He had his familiar place; it was positioned perfectly to lie in comfort while keeping a watchful eye for the family to come home until he tuckered out and fell asleep.

With the exception of a grumpy cat on occasion—most likely from some rough play, since no one was home to suggest otherwise—Vinnie had the run of the house, and it was surprisingly uneventful.

## Favorite Spots

We all shared our own times and activities with Vinnie. He had us trained the way he wanted us. He enjoyed each of us for those special times and spots he frequented.

Late-afternoon and after-dinner naps were spent with my husband on the recliner. We had to keep a blanket on the chair because Vinnie always wanted to be under cover and it was mandatory that my husband attend as well. The chair was a bit tight for the both of them; plus, Vinnie would run and jump into place and wait patiently for company when it was nap time. The chair took a beating and eventually Santa had to bring them an oversized recliner so they could snuggle in comfort.

When it was my daughter's turn for a snuggle, Vinnie got first dibs on his favorite spot under the covers of her bed. She would often wake in some cramped contortion around a very comfortable Vinnie. Vinnie didn't mind but, again, Santa needed to bring a bigger bed.

Bedtime was a ritual as well. I already admitted we allowed Vinnie to sleep in our bed. Again, he took his position all the way under the covers at the foot of the bed. The winters in western New York can be quite blustery, so heavier comforters and covers were needed but had to be positioned so Vinnie could have easy access in and out from his burrow. We often found ourselves clutching the edges of the bed while a very happy, warm Dalmatian was stretched out in the middle.

When we introduced a new dog bed for Vinnie to utilize when the family was not readily available for under-cover encounters, he was not overly enthusiastic or interested. We tried treats and positive reinforcement, but he was not pleased. I noticed that during the times that Vinnie would be sitting on my bed, not-so-patiently waiting for us to join him, he positioned himself on a furry coverlet that I kept there. Could it really be that simple? It was. I purchased Vinnie his own furry coverlet for his bed. Vinnie was so pleased that we would often find him sound asleep, all four legs straight up in the air, on his furry blanket on his bed.

Maybe it sounds silly that we would allow the dog to control so many things, but in reality they were simple things that we enjoyed as much as Vinnie did. Of course, Vinnie still preferred to be touching a family member, but we were able to give him comfort places to both share with us and to keep as his favorite spots when we were not available. We were his people and he was one of us, so we happily made these changes for him because we loved him lots!

## Stranger Danger

Sometime during Vinnie's second year, something changed.

I mentioned earlier the warning about how a deaf dog's personality can shift unexpectedly, and violent tendencies can present themselves. We thought, since the warning timeframe had come and gone, we had dodged that bullet. Vinnie had been great with all people and all dogs, even strangers. We were not sure what happened or why, but, seemingly all of a sudden, Vinnie became very wary of strangers. We all watched him closely, since, with Vinnie, there was a reason for everything. All actions required reactions. Thanks to our unique perceptions with him, we definitely took notice of the changes.

His personality change was subtle in the beginning; it was hardly noticeable. Vinnie enjoyed riding in the car. He was used to wearing his seatbelt and sitting like a gentleman in the back seat. He did not run around or act silly. He knew his place and respected it. He always had an aristocratic appearance on his face as he rode, and it was good fun for those who passed us. He was a good-looking dog who was proud to be sitting in his car. It made me smile to watch him. Except for one situation as a pup with the swirling paper outside his day-care center, he did not react much to outside stimuli except—for an occasional greeting to a squirrel or passing dog.

People did not bother him, either.

Gradually, that began to change. He began to bark uncontrollably if someone walked too close to the car.

Vinnie loved when the UPS delivery man dropped off a package. The UPS man always kept special treats for Vinnie in his truck and knew to watch for him as he drove down the driveway due to Vinnie's deafness. Vinnie enjoyed his visits. Vinnie was never outside unless one of us was home, and these kind of visits were always used as part of our positive reinforcement training. It was important to keep Vinnie socialized, both with people and other animals.

One day, my husband noticed that when Vinnie saw the UPS truck coming down the driveway, instead of his usual, wiggly excited self, he was barking and nervous. It was the same truck, but it was a different driver. Vinnie wanted no part of this new guy, even without meeting him. My husband intervened and attempted to work through the situation but was uncomfortable with the change in Vinnie's attitude. Vinnie was put in the house. We have always been of the mindset that a dog's judgment of character should be taken very seriously. They just seem to know. Maybe this was an isolated situation, but it prompted us to carefully watch for future visits, whether it was this driver or not.

Another time, my daughter had friends over, and they were watching television, just hanging out. Vinnie was with them. All seemed fine until one of the boys in the group—a boy who had not been to the house before—changed the position of his hat or moved in a certain way. I am not sure exactly what happened, but Vinnie reacted with a cautionary warning. He did not try to bite, but he stood in front of the boy and would not break eye contact. It was a warning stance that could have become more. Vinnie was told to stand down, and he was removed from the situation. We were all noticing a change in him. He had never acted like this before.

Not long after these incidents, I was picking Vinnie up from day care one afternoon when another uncomfortable episode occurred. Vinnie usually emerged from his play area to receive a treat and put his seat belt on to go home. The day began normally, but while I was paying the bill, a lady in the receiving area walked over to him and held her hand out to him. Vinnie grabbed at her coat sleeve. He did not try to bite her. It was not really done in a threatening way, but it was out of character for him just the same. The day care owner also saw it happen. He commented that the lady had walked into his space and was in the way of his treat. She had interfered with his routine. That was most likely very true, but that, plus his behavior with my daughter's friend, plus the UPS situation, made me more concerned. Something was changing.

I used this last turn of events to discuss my concerns with the owners of the day care. Since they were dog trainers themselves and worked closely with many dogs each day, I trusted their instincts. They had not seen any changes in Vinnie during his stays with them, but they wondered if, because he was becoming an adult, he was taking his leadership role in the family very seriously and felt the need to protect the family member he was with.

Vinnie was protecting us . . . That made sense. What we did not understand was, why then? Like people, animals go through hormone changes, and we all know sometimes it is handled well, and sometimes, not so much.

Vinnie was fine with anyone he knew, no differences in his behavior whatsoever. It was the unknown that agitated him.

## For the Love of Vinnie!

Vinnie was changing before our eyes—and not in a good way. We now had to be cautious whenever a stranger came into contact with Vinnie. We were very careful and observant of *all* of Vinnie's actions, not just the new ones. His OCD tendencies were also becoming more persistent. Reflections, shadows, anything. It all seemed to really bother him more than ever.

At this point, we were afraid he was going to become violent. You can be careful and you can be cautious, but it seems that sometimes, no matter what you do, you can never prevent everything bad from happening. Vinnie was having stranger danger issues, but he had been fine with those he knew . . . or so we thought.

One afternoon, a neighbor came to the house on his riding lawnmower. Vinnie was outside with my husband, and the neighbor extended his hand to Vinnie, which Vinnie promptly took a bite out of.

Oh, gosh! Doggone it, Vinnie! He had passed the point of no return this time.

The neighbor was fine, and he was beside himself with blame. He felt that it was his fault—he had startled Vinnie by being on the running, moving lawnmower at the time. I am sure that was part of it, but I explained we could no longer harbor any more excuses. Vinnie was transitioning into a new behavior pattern that was problematic. How quickly memories of our first year came flooding back.

We accepted in stride the ten-day quarantine "house arrest" customary with any dog bite. Vinnie now added "convict" to his laundry list of issues as well as "mean" dog. We thought we were doing so well, but we now had a new hurdle to scale.

I was referred to a trainer who specialized in behavior modification in extreme cases. We were not sure Vinnie was an *extreme* case yet, but we really did not want to take any chances of him becoming one. We had come such a long way and had overcome so many obstacles. Surely, we could figure something out with help.

I made the call to what I now understand was considered a "behavior boot camp." I had heard the term before but did not really understand it. Nor did I understand what exactly "behavior modification" really meant or the methods used to obtain such change.

In the movies, before people deliver bad news, they always ask, "Are you are sitting down?" I will admit, this was cause for me to sit down.

The consultant I spoke to was harsh at best and sounded very much like a drill sergeant. Without even knowing me, she immediately gave me a terse scolding and a guilt complex that I had allowed my dog to get to this point. She flat-out said that their facility was my only hope, now that my dog had tasted blood.

I was definitely sitting down by that point, and I was completely speechless. Once she had finished making me feel like a complete failure—which I am sure is part of their program—I gave her the details of Vinnie's case and the steps we had taken. She didn't care. She was unwavering on the program's requirements, regardless of Vinnie's disabilities.

The program was a minimum of six weeks of in-house containment, more if deemed necessary. I would drop the dog off and not have any visitation with him for the entire length of the program. They would notify me when they felt he was ready to come home.

I was overwhelmed. This was so extreme, and, needless to say, the cost was also extreme. I explained that I had many questions on what techniques they used and what experience they had with deaf dogs. She bluntly told me that it didn't matter if he was deaf or not. She was sure their methods would work. He would behave when he got home. When I asked if I could speak to the trainer I'd been referred to, I was told no. I was *not* allowed to speak to the trainer—he was very busy, and this was the program. Did I want to sign up or not?

Um . . . *No, thank you*!

It's possible that I was overreacting to this program, but I did not like what I was hearing. I was looking for help with Vinnie's fear of strangers—I was not looking for a "Stepford" dog that had been scared or punished into submission. I did not want a perfect dog. I wanted Vinnie. I just did not want Vinnie to bite people. Over a month without his family was enough to discourage me without all the details, given how alone and scared he was when he couldn't see us. So we needed a Plan B.

I went back to my Rolodex and began calling trainers. I received many suggestions and offers, but most just did not sound like what we needed. We did not need more classes; we needed some individual, specific training. I will say, all were in agreement that the boot camp option was overly extreme for a dog that had not fully developed this behavior yet and had only bitten once. How do you correct behavior when you don't even completely understand the precipitating factors?

I spoke with one of the trainers who had been willing to allow us to join her classes. I explained our new plight, and she immediately had some amazing ideas. She offered to come to the house as a stranger and witness Vinnie's reaction. We would work with her individually in the very environment that was causing our issues.

She asked us to put Vinnie on his leash inside the house. She came to the door, and we watched his reaction play out. He was a bit confused that he was on a leash in the house, but everyone needed to be safe, and none of us knew for sure how he would act.

When the trainer came to the door, Vinnie aggressively barked at her. He did not bare teeth, lunge, or attempt to bite, but it was obvious that he was uncomfortable with her being there. He would not settle and would not break eye contact with her, even for treats. Oh, don't get me wrong, he would take the treat—but she was not supposed to be there, and he knew it.

He was nervous and conflicted about what he should do. I don't think he wanted to be mean. He just didn't know the correct way to respond in his new role as protector.

The trainer was great with Vinnie and was calm and collected throughout the entire session. Eventually, she had us take Vinnie off the leash. He continued to bark, but she pointed out where he was standing and his body language as he was barking. He was actually standing *behind* us, barking but not approaching her. She was paying him no attention, but she was a stranger in his house. It was apparent that he was more fussed about the fact that *she* was not fussed by him.

That was our first lesson. If nothing else, it was a great relief to know that our dog was not a lost cause. Much of this was normal, growing, adolescent-to-adult dog behavior as they struggled with the duty of protecting their families. Though not acceptable behavior, it was not a hopeless cause.

We were given homework, and she visited us weekly for a few weeks. Each time she came, Vinnie acted unhappy that she was there, but he immediately nudged her pocket where the treats were kept. He was playing hard to get. I believe I saw that silly smile of his whenever he saw her car arrive. We made some good progress working with him, thanks to her help. We would never let our guard down or allow him to be unattended when someone arrived, but we became far more comfortable reading the signs he was showing us, as well as appreciating some of the markers that led to his aggressive behavior.

We are not sure why, but he did not like when someone offered their hand to him. That motion seemed to incense him for some reason. If the visitor came to the house, went about their business, and simply ignored him, he eventually became curious enough to stop misbehaving and approach cautiously. We could work with that. We just needed to be vigilant and to warn people not to offer their hand, even though offering a hand to smell is the most common thing people do when meeting a new dog.

We live in a very rural area, and we do not have many unexpected visitors at the house. That helped us a great deal. I also became very proficient at tracking my UPS packages, too. Whenever I was expecting a package and could track it to the date, I made sure Vinnie attended day care that day. It worked.

Vinnie was our guy. He was the most loving, playful dog, and he was working so hard to please us. He just did not understand how to harness this need to protect us. We needed to stay one step ahead of whatever he threw at us. We had to find a creative way to communicate right from wrong.

Several of the trainers we had spoken to suggested we invest in a shock-type collar. We were not receptive to this in the beginning, but given how effective and humane the invisible fence was, we realized it might not be a bad idea. It, like the fence, was a training tool that Vinnie would learn to respect if used correctly. It needed to be used as a training tool—not a punishment factor.

With a little research, we learned that collars are available that are geared toward deaf dogs. You can offer multiple levels of vibration or shock via a remote control, ranging from a tickle to a decent zap on a one to one hundred scale. As with the fence, we all tested the levels on ourselves. I would never be comfortable with any method I hadn't experienced personally. The very low levels were no more than a tickle.

The collar worked. We found the level that he could feel without hurting him, and we worked with him on some of the stubborn behaviors we had previously been unsuccessful at preventing, like bothering the cat, getting on the kitchen counters, and other bad manners. As with any dog, you need to catch them right in the act and react immediately for them to understand that it is that particular behavior that is unacceptable. For most, a good, old-fashioned shout or verbal warning would do the trick. We were at a disadvantage and unable to do that with Vinnie. Hand signals worked great if we had his attention—not so great if we didn't. The vibration feature also allowed us to call him back when he could not see us. If he was out in the yard or in another part of the house, we had a code with the vibration that meant "come find us."

He responded extremely well to all of this training. In fact, after a while, we did not even need the collar anymore. If he was being naughty or not paying attention, we just needed to show him the remote, and he would cooperate.

We were making progress again and heading in a good direction, even with our setbacks. Year two was back on track and looking up.

## Returning the Favor

Pet families love their pets. We try to give them everything we have to give, and we do our best to make them full-fledged family members. Often, we talk about what we give to them, the sacrifices we make for them, but what they give back to us is easily taken for granted.

Unconditional love is a beautiful concept, but do we really know what that means? Vinnie needed us, and we responded. We needed Vinnie, and he returned the favor!

As I look back over the craziness the past two years had afforded us, I could see as many laughs as I could see tears. There were victories right alongside the losses, but at the end of the day, there was a cold, wet nose attached to a heart that beat just to be with us and to please us.

One of my biggest pet peeves is when people have a pet just to have a pet—not really caring for that pet the way it needs. The stories I read and knew to be true from personal encounters through volunteer work sometimes broke my heart. Folks would go and either buy or adopt a dog, then turn around and immediately return it, since it was not what they wanted. Hearing statements like "it's too much work" or "I don't want to make that much effort" made me what to scream. Why the heck did you get a dog?! What did you think it was going to be like? Please don't get another one! Want to know how I really feel?

Sorry about that. This is a total soap box issue for another discussion.

When we accepted Vinnie into our lives, we had no idea the amount of time commitment or the hurdles we would face. But we did know that you do not take on a pet unless you are willing to devote time and energy to that pet, regardless.

Vinnie was a team sport. We all became part of his life, we all shared in his care, and we all received the benefits of his attention and love. Vinnie loved the heck out of all of us, too!

The summer that Vinnie came to live with us was a transition time for my daughter. She had just graduated from college. She needed to study and prepare for her medical boards, search for the perfect job, and enter into her new career. She took on the day shift with Vinnie that summer. She and Vinnie studied, took "selfies," learned new tricks, and played. Vinnie kept her grounded, made her take breaks when she needed them, and was happy to sit and study with her. She loved being home with him, and it benefitted her so much because Vinnie's schedule afforded her the time to do the prep work she needed to prepare for her future.

If Vinnie had not been there, I am sure she would have done just fine, but it seemed to work out perfectly for both of them. She not only achieved her goals but landed an amazing job. I firmly believe that Vinnie had a hand in her success. Vinnie just wanted to be doing whatever you were doing, as long as he could do it with you.

The winter of Vinnie's second year, my mother needed to stay with us for a few months to help her gain control of some health issues. She took the day shift with Vinnie during that time. Vinnie was happy to have his grandmother stay. Vinnie would get up and complete his morning routines with us, and as soon as we were ready to leave for work, off to Gramma's room he went to get in an extra nap and a snuggle. My mother had to quickly learn the "no closed doors" policy.

Vinnie was active, and he made my mother get active too, which was exactly what she needed. He made her get up and walk to let him out to chase the squirrel. He made her get up and feed him lunch. He made her do what she needed to do, and he loved her and attended to her all the while. I am not sure she even realized that she was doing as much as she was doing. It didn't matter. Vinnie needed her to do it, so she did it willingly.

I would say, by the end of her stay with us, Vinnie could boast a pretty good success record with his grandmother as well as with my daughter. She gained back the strength she needed from all the walking she was doing, and enjoyed sharing as much attention as Vinnie. They both thrived.

Vinnie's vet was an amazing part of Vinnie's life as well—not just for surgically removing his mistakes but for being involved and helping us to master whatever Vinnie threw at us. All the calls we made were met with patient, reassuring assistance, even if she didn't really know or when she needed to clean up the messes of others. After all, as I mentioned before, Vinnie never seemed to get sick during normal business hours.

Vinnie's vet also helped us plan his routines and care. At one point, she showed me that she had elected to focus her continuing education credits that year on the ingestion of foreign objects in dogs in honor of Vinnie. She certainly got enough clinical practice on the subject thanks to Vinnie, but it also benefitted us that she was willing to learn everything she could to help us.

Vinnie was our guy. He was there for us. Whatever we wanted or needed to do, he was fine with it. He had his favorite spots and activities with each of us. Vinnie shared nap time. He would share our shadows with us. He could make us crazy, but he always made us laugh and sometimes cry. We loved that silly dog!

Each time we shared a success or a hurdle, we rejoiced. Each setback, we cried. Each birthday that we shared, we celebrated. Vinnie was a gift.

## What Goes Up Must Come Down

We celebrated birthday number three with an adorable iced doggie bone sent home especially for Vinnie from the pet shop where I purchased his food. Everyone who knew Vinnie shared in his life. He touched so many of us in so many ways. He happily gobbled it down, opened his gifts, and was a happy guy for the rest of the day. We made it to year three!

I suppose you have probably reasoned by now that my story has a sad twist of fate. The use of past tense throughout my stories was a giveaway, I am sure. I promised not to make you cry, but, unfortunately, our story does not have the happy ending we all hoped for.

About a week after Vinnie's third birthday, he began randomly throwing up. He was still eating and drinking, so it was not the previous telltale signs that he had a blockage from eating something he was not supposed to. All toys were accounted for, and nothing unusual seemed to be missing. All dogs experience gastric issues from time to time. Vinnie was no exception to that rule, but given his past issues, we were overly sensitive to anything with him. It was a trained response.

It continued for a day or so, and then it appeared to clear up. Vinnie seemed to be feeling all right. He just had a bad belly. We watched him closely.

Part of living with a dog with Pica is "poop patrol." At the end of each week, poop needed to be picked up from the yard and counted. This was a good way to be sure that what was being eaten was being processed appropriately. That is the nicest way I can explain it. Whenever there were suspect times, that weekly poop patrol became daily. We needed to make sure he was indeed having a bowel movement but also that there wasn't anything in that movement that did not belong. In this case, everything on that end seemed to be in order as well.

The tummy troubles appeared to return in a week or so. Vinnie vomited randomly in intervals again. It was not happening after each meal or even every day, but it was happening more regularly than it should be. We called the vet. She examined him and could hear normal digestive sounds. He seemed to be feeling his usual bad self. He did not have a fever, and he was passing what he ate, other than what he threw up. Vinnie was put on a prescription bland diet to help clear up whatever was bothering him. He did well on the bland diet, albeit begrudgingly.

A few days later, I picked Vinnie up from day care in the afternoon to a report that Vinnie had not wanted to eat his lunch. This was cause for alarm. Remember, Vinnie's favorite time of day was meal time, bland diet or not.

The vomiting was back, and this time it was a bit more aggressive. It seemed like Vinnie wanted to eat. He was hungry, but he just couldn't eat. We called the vet. She called us back immediately but, unfortunately, informed us apologetically that she was out of town for a few days. That seemed to be our motto all the way through Vinnie's life. We did not feel that the issue was life-threatening, since he was drinking and seemed to want to play; he just didn't want to eat. We scheduled an appointment in a few days.

My husband called me the following day very upset. He had gone home for lunch, and Vinnie was just not Vinnie. He had stopped drinking, did not seem to be able to pass a bowel movement, and didn't want to chase his shadow. But most of all, he seemed sad.

I appreciate how that must sound, but to know Vinnie, this was a significant change. He was never sad! In fact, he was the happiest dog we had ever encountered. My husband felt that Vinnie was not in a good place, and he was concerned about waiting for our vet to return. I called an emergency clinic that was near Vinnie's day care. I explained our situation, drove home, and loaded up Vinnie and his medical records. Off we went.

We were met with very kind and thorough care at the ER. They took us immediately, and the vet was a gentle man who listened intently as I explained Vinnie's history. He examined him and could immediately feel a mass in his abdomen. He could not tell what it was from this initial examination, but we knew the drill by this point. Vinnie would be admitted, and he would be sedated and X-rayed.

I signed the forms and left my sweet dog in good hands, but the foreboding feeling I had as I left was almost more than I could bear. We had done so well as a family. What did we miss?

How did we end up back at this point? Which family member had left something smaller than a beach towel within his reach?

The ER vet called and verified what we already knew. Vinnie had a mass in his abdomen that was not allowing food to make it through his intestines. He could not tell from the X-ray what that mass was, so Vinnie was scheduled for surgery the following morning. He was sedated and hydrated and was able to rest comfortably until they could remove the source of his plight. The plan was for the vet to call me the next afternoon during his office hours and give me an update on Vinnie's condition.

The clinic was very close to my office, so I went to work like I normally would. I was hoping to bring Vinnie home later that day after his surgery, so I cleared my schedule to be able to stay with him for a few days post-surgery. I had gotten rather proficient at this task over the course of the past three years. I had not been at work very long that morning when my phone rang. The caller ID was the vet clinic. It was not my scheduled call time. I did not want to answer that call!

Honestly, I heard very little after the first few sentences of that conversation. The vet had actually left surgery to call me due to what he'd found. Vinnie was still on the operating table.

After hearing the words, "Mrs. Artieri, it is not good," the rest of the conversation might as well have been a sound bite from a Charlie Brown cartoon, with the "wah wah, wah-wah wah" that represented the teacher's voice.

The mass was not a blockage at all. It was a large tumor approximately the size of a baseball, positioned at the base of Vinnie's stomach and blocking the food from emptying from the stomach to his intestines. The doctor felt it must have been a very fast-growing tumor that hadn't completely blocked the flow of food until right at the end. That explained why he only threw up intermittently.

Vinnie's abdomen was a mess. He had many adhesions from his multiple surgeries, and there were some areas of questionable scarring, most likely from our issue with the second ER clinic surgeon. The cancer was also visible in other places as well. This time, it was not his fault at all. It was none of our faults. There was nothing that we could have done to prevent this.

Cancer takes many beloved pets. Vinnie was obviously beginning to suffer. We had to let him go. With everything we had tried, everyone we had spoken to who helped us, with every ounce of effort we had given, in the end, we could not save him. Vinnie was humanely euthanatized on the operating table that morning.

As I drove home that day, after picking up all Vinnie's worldly possessions from the clinic and saying my farewell to my beautiful boy, I was devastated. Vinnie was so full of life one minute, and the next, he was gone.

It was a warm day full of sunshine, and, driving with my windows down, I found a calm place in my mind. I found the strength to accept that, in Vinnie's world, everything was black and white—and I am not referencing his coat. He had done exceptionally well trying to fit into our world, but he just could not quite make it.

# Everything Happens for a Reason

I will admit, there is an emptiness in our home now that's about the size of the state of Texas! Vinnie was our life. His bell still hangs from the front door. No one wants to remove it.

I will say, we all seem to have a great deal more free time these days. I am back to that "I'm never doing it again" phase, but we all know I most likely will again, at some point. The question is, would I take on another deaf or special needs dog? Yes, I believe I would, as long as my family is willing and I am able to offer them as much care as they need.

Because family always comes first to us, we needed to tie up some loose ends. We chose to send communication to the second vet about our findings once Vinnie passed. We never knew for sure they were to blame until they opened him the last time, but we continued to be very upset at the treatment Vinnie received while in their care. We did not expect much to come of it, but felt it important to relay the information to them to hopefully prevent another animal from experiencing what Vinnie did. I wrote a very comprehensive letter outlining all the details and our concerns. It was met with a very apologetic office manager and a very argumentative surgeon, who called my home a few times to rehash my claims repeatedly. An attorney friend wrote a letter on our behalf asking them to refund our money to help offset the cost of the vet bills we had to pay to fix the issues they caused. They refused to acknowledge any accountability for what happened, but instead sent the request to the malpractice insurance company to handle. The outcome of their decision was discouraging. The malpractice insurance company came to the conclusion that we could not prove that all of Vinnie's complications were solely caused by their client, so they were denying our claim. We did ask that even though they might not agree on the sole ownership of the malpractice, did we not illustrate a thorough display of the lack of ethics on their part? The response to that statement was equally as discouraging. Ethics were an irrelevant part to both the insurance company and the veterinary practice. We were told if we wished to pursue our claim, we could file a lawsuit. We had fought the good fight for Vinnie, but a lawsuit was not going to bring him back. We buried our claims with our beautiful Vinnie.

I put pen to paper to recount our time with Vinnie because I want to share, with whoever will listen to our stories, just how special our time together was. Not all deaf dogs will develop other issues like Vinnie; he, for some reason, was given a full bag of tricks.

I want people to understand, though, that special needs animals are not "throwaway" animals. They can lead quality lives and enrich ours so much, if people are willing to invest time and care for them. There are many amazing folks out there trying to do just that.

The premise of my story has to be a firm realization that loving and caring for a special needs animal is extremely doable. It is doable, but it is not something that should be done by just anyone. You have to be willing to make the commitment to that animal completely. It cannot be a try-it-and-see situation; these animals learn to trust and depend on you.

A special needs animal does not always have the same resilience as a normal animal, and without the security that they need, it can be extremely frustrating for all involved. There are so many animals that end up being abandoned in dog rings or relinquished to shelters because people cannot or will not commit.

You also cannot do it alone. You will need help. Never be afraid to reach out for help when you need it. If you have the means, the ability, and the desire to help an animal, then please do it. There really are no right or wrong answers, as long as you have the best interest of the animal in mind. Never give up on them, even when they seem hopeless. There is a heart beating in them that you must find the right way to capture.

We only had three short years with Vinnie, but they were happy ones. Vinnie enjoyed his life, and he brought us an abundance of joy. I hope you enjoyed the story of Vinnie and my family. I hope we motivated you to be a bit more patient with your animals, whether special needs or not. I would not be truthful if I did not admit how many times I wanted to give up or how many times I cried, not knowing what to do. But, in the end, we asked for help where we could find it, and we just figured it out. We loved Vinnie lots, and that was enough!

My name is Kelly. I owned a Dalmatian named Vinnie. Vinnie was deaf. When Vinnie left, he left an empty spot in my heart and changed my life forever!

# References & Resources

Encyclopedia of Veterinary Terms. Retrieved from http://www.petmd.com/veterinaryterms

Strand, P., & Strand, R. (1995). *The Dalmatian: An Owner's Guide to a Happy Healthy Pet*. New York, NY: Howell Book House.

Coile, C. (2014, February 28). The Problem with Merle Coat Pattern in Dogs. Retrieved from http://www.dogster.com/lifestyle/dog-breeds-breeding-merle-patterns

Strain, G. (1999). Congenital Deafness and Its Recognition. *Veterinary Clinics of North America: Small Animal Practice, 29*(4), 895-907. doi:10.1016/s0195-5616(99)50079-x

Benal, J. (2011, November 29). Pica: Eating Things That Aren't Food. Retrieved from http://www.quickanddirtytips.com/pets/dog-behavior/pica-eating-things-that-arent-food

Deaf Dog Education Action Fund: http://www.deafdogs.org/

Deaf Dogs Blog: deafdogs@yahoogroups.com

American Kennel Club: http://www.akc.org/

Dalmatian Club of America: http://www.thedca.org/

## Special Thanks

∙ ∙ ∙ ∙ ∙ ∙ ∙ ∙ ∙ ∙ ∙ ∙ ∙ ∙ ∙ ∙ ∙ ∙ ∙ ∙ ∙ ∙ ∙ ∙ ∙ ∙ ∙ ∙ ∙ ∙ ∙ ∙ ∙ ∙ ∙ ∙ ∙ ∙ ∙ ∙ ∙ ∙ ∙ ∙ ∙ ∙ ∙ ∙

Dr. Mary Neilens

Dr. Robert Harper

Grand Island Pet Lodge

Grand Island Small Animal Hospital

Greater Buffalo Veterinary Emergency Clinic

Karen Drumm – Harmony Dog Training

Sue McNaught of Celtic Canines

Liz Grewal – deafdogs@yahoogroups.com

All Dawgs Academy

Melissa Cimra & family – Firemark Dalmatians

Sandra Stadtmueller

Brian Hutchison, Esq.

www.ingramcontent.com/pod-product-compliance
Lightning Source LLC
Chambersburg PA
CBHW041958080526
44588CB00021B/2791